ADHD and Other Behavior Disorders

LIVING WITH DISEASES AND DISORDERS

ADHD and Other Behavior Disorders

JOHN PERRITANO

SERIES ADVISOR
HEATHER L. PELLETIER, Ph.D.

Pediatric Psychologist, Hasbro Children's Hospital
Clinical Assistant Professor, Warren Alpert Medical School of Brown University

MASON CREST

Mason Crest
450 Parkway Drive, Suite D
Broomall, PA 19008
www.masoncrest.com

MTM Publishing, Inc.
435 West 23rd Street, #8C
New York, NY 10011
www.mtmpublishing.com

President: Valerie Tomaselli
Vice President, Book Development: Hilary Poole
Designer: Annemarie Redmond
Copyeditor: Peter Jaskowiak
Editorial Assistant: Leigh Eron

Series ISBN: 978-1-4222-3747-2
Hardback ISBN: 978-1-4222-3748-9
E-Book ISBN: 978-1-4222-8029-4

Library of Congress Cataloging-in-Publication Data
Names: Perritano, John, author.
Title: ADHD and other behavior disorders / by John Perritano.
Description: Broomall, PA: Mason Crest, [2018] | Series: Living with
   diseases and disorders | Includes index.
Identifiers: LCCN 2017009918 (print) | LCCN 2017010719 (ebook) | ISBN
   9781422237489 (hardback: alk. paper) | ISBN 9781422280294 (ebook)
Subjects: LCSH: Attention-deficit hyperactivity disorder. | Attention-deficit
   hyperactivity disorder—Treatment.
Classification: LCC RJ506.H9 P47 2018 (print) | LCC RJ506.H9 (ebook) | DDC
   618.92/8589—dc23
LC record available at https://lccn.loc.gov/2017009918

Printed and bound in the United States of America.

First printing
9 8 7 6 5 4 3 2 1

TABLE OF CONTENTS

Key Icons to Look for:

 Words to Understand: These words with their easy-to-understand definitions will increase the reader's understanding of the text, while building vocabulary skills.

 Sidebars: This boxed material within the main text allows readers to build knowledge, gain insights, explore possibilities, and broaden their perspectives by weaving together additional information to provide realistic and holistic perspectives.

 Educational Videos: Readers can view videos by scanning our QR codes, which will provide them with additional educational content to supplement the text. Examples include news coverage, moments in history, speeches, iconic sports moments, and much more.

 Text-Dependent Questions: These questions send the reader back to the text for more careful attention to the evidence presented there.

 Research Projects: Readers are pointed toward areas of further inquiry connected to each chapter. Suggestions are provided for projects that encourage deeper research and analysis.

 Series Glossary of Key Terms: This back-of-the-book glossary contains terminology used throughout the series. Words found here increase the reader's ability to read and comprehend higher-level books and articles in this field.

SERIES INTRODUCTION

According to the Chronic Disease Center at the Centers for Disease Control and Prevention, over 100 million Americans suffer from a chronic illness or medical condition. In other words, they have a health problem that lasts three months or more, affects their ability to perform normal activities, and requires frequent medical care and/or hospitalizations. Epidemiological studies suggest that between 15 and 18 million of those with chronic illness or medical conditions are children and adolescents. That's roughly one out of every four children in the United States.

These young people must exert more time and energy to complete the tasks their peers do with minimal thought. For example, kids with Crohn's disease, ulcerative colitis, or other digestive issues have to plan meals and snacks carefully, to make sure they are not eating food that could irritate their stomachs or cause pain and discomfort. People with cerebral palsy, muscular dystrophy, or other physical limitations associated with a medical condition may need help getting dressed, using the bathroom, or joining an activity in gym class. Those with cystic fibrosis, asthma, or epilepsy may have to avoid certain activities or environments altogether. ADHD and other behavior disorders require the individual to work harder to sustain the level of attention and focus necessary to keep up in school.

Living with a chronic illness or medical condition is not easy. Identifying a diagnosis and adjusting to the initial shock is only the beginning of a long journey. Medications, follow-up appointments and procedures, missed school or work, adjusting to treatment regimens, coping with uncertainty, and readjusting expectations are all hurdles one has to overcome in learning how to live one's best life. Naturally, feelings of sadness or anxiety may set in while learning how to make it all work. This is especially true for young people, who may reach a point in their medical journey when they have to rethink some of their original goals and life plans to better match their health reality.

Chances are, you know people who live this reality on a regular basis. It is important to remember that those affected by chronic illness are family members, neighbors, friends, or maybe even our own doctors. They are likely navigating the demands of the day a little differently, as they balance the specific accommodations necessary to manage their illness. But they have the same desire to be productive and included as those who are fortunate not to have a chronic illness.

This set provides valuable information about the most common childhood chronic illnesses, in language that is engaging and easy for students to grasp. Each chapter highlights important vocabulary words and offers text-dependent questions to help assess comprehension. Meanwhile, educational videos (available by scanning QR codes) and research projects help connect the text to the outside world.

Our mission with this set is twofold. First, the volumes provide a go-to source for information about chronic illness for young people who are living with particular conditions. Each volume in this set strives to provide reliable medical information and practical advice for living day-to-day with various challenges. Second, we hope these volumes will also help kids without chronic illness better understand and appreciate how people with health challenges live. After all, if one in four young people is managing a health condition, it's safe to assume that the majority of our youth already know someone with a chronic illness, whether they realize it or not.

With the growing presence of social media, bullying is easier than ever before. It's vital that young people take a moment to stop and think about how they are more similar to kids with health challenges than they are different. Poor understanding and low tolerance for individual differences are often the platforms for bullying and noninclusive behavior, both in person and online. Living with Diseases and Disorders strives to close the gap of misunderstanding.

The ultimate solution to the bullying problem is surely an increase in empathy. We hope these books will help readers better understand and appreciate not only the daily struggles of people living with chronic conditions, but their triumphs as well.

—Heather Pelletier, Ph.D.
Hasbro Children's Hospital
Warren Alpert Medical School of Brown University

WORDS TO UNDERSTAND

hyperactivity: the condition of being extremely active.

impulsive: doing something rash without thinking it through.

maelstrom: a powerful storm with whirling winds or seas.

manifest: to display the symptoms of a condition, often in the sense of an emotional state (e.g., to manifest signs of anxiety).

mercurial: subject to unpredictable mood changes.

CHAPTER ONE

What Is ADHD?

When Kerri MacKay is in class, she feels like a "pinball." She can't focus. She can't concentrate. She describes the feeling as "bouncing from one thing to another." In her blog, she writes, "There are no windows and my gaze drifts toward the orange door of my classroom. My foot bounces up and down, and my attention pings around during the lecture. . . . My professor is speaking just a few feet away, but he fades in and out of my focus."

Kerri's attention shifts between the presentation and the notes she's taking on her computer. She hears a bit of laughter from other students, yet her mind drifts, like a rudderless ship meandering on a dark stormy ocean. "This isn't a boring class. . . . I want to pay attention. . . . But I'm caught up in the chaos of the sounds of my fellow students—zippers, coughs, pens, keyboard clicks. . . . This is just a snippet of what ADHD looks, sounds, and feels like to me."

Kerri is not alone. According to the Centers for Disease Control and Prevention (CDC), 11 percent of children between the ages of 4 and 17 suffer from attention-deficit/hyperactivity disorder (ADHD). Although symptoms can differ somewhat from person to person, ADHD is characterized by inattentiveness, **hyperactivity**, and **impulsive** behavior. The condition usually begins in childhood, but teens and adults can also have ADHD.

"Having [ADHD] is like having a turbocharged race-car brain," writes Edward M. Hallowell and John J. Ratey, authors of *Delivered from Distraction: Getting the Most out of Life with Attention Deficit Disorder.* "The core symptoms . . . are excessive distractibility, impulsivity, and restlessness. These can lead both children and adults to underachieve at school, at work, in relationships and marriage, and in all other settings."

Boys are more than twice as likely as girls to be diagnosed with ADHD.

ADHD BY THE NUMBERS

According to the National Health Interview Survey 2011–2013, which reports a on a wide range of health topics in the United States, 9.5 percent of children ages 4 to 17 were diagnosed with ADHD during that period. Out of that number:

- 2.7 percent were between the ages of 4 and 5.
- 9.5 percent were between the ages of 6 and 11.
- 11.8 percent were between the ages of 12 and 17.

People with ADHD may find it difficult to turn ideas into actions. They sometimes have a hard time explaining their thought processes to others. Some are chronic underachievers who flounder in school, work, or personal relationships, while others are quite driven and achieve at a high level. But regardless of their success, having ADHD causes a lot of frustration, and people who have to deal with it are often moody and angry.

Interestingly, some people with ADHD are creative and are applauded for thinking "outside the box" and finding creative solutions to perplexing problems. They look at life from an unusual perspective and have remarkable strength. Celebrities such as the performer Justin Timberlake, business tycoon Richard Branson, and actor Will Smith all have ADHD. Some

EDUCATIONAL VIDEO

Scan this code for a video about people who have thrived with ADHD.

Justin Timberlake in 2016. Timberlake has publicly discussed his struggles with ADHD.

historians believe that the **mercurial** Theodore Roosevelt, the 26th president of the United States, also had ADHD, although the condition was not known in its current form at the time.

Where's the Off Button?

People who have ADHD say it feels as though their brains don't shut off. Their minds bounce from one thought to another, like the pinball that Kerri described. Kids might fidget and squirm when they are sitting down. They might constantly get up from their seat, or bolt across a room. People with ADHD sometimes describe themselves as always "on the go."

Teens and adults with ADHD might feel restless, impatient, or have a hard time waiting to say what's on their minds. "It is as if a person with ADHD is driving through thick fog, on a dark road, trying to get to where they know they are supposed to be. The problem is, you lost the directions and have no GPS to guide you — and, in the background, the radio is playing loud songs that are changing," one ADHD sufferer wrote on a website for those with ADHD. Another says ADHD feels "like I am drowning in a **maelstrom** of stuff that needs to get done, but that I never finish. It's like a never-ending feeling of futility."

 ## SIGNS AND SYMPTOMS

We've said that people with ADHD display inattention, hyperactivity, and impulsivity. But what does that mean in a practical sense?

People who are inattentive often

- make careless mistakes at work or school,
- don't listen when someone is speaking,
- have a hard time following instructions,
- are disorganized,
- are easily distracted,
- are always losing things, and
- are forgetful.

Hyperactivity is another aspect of ADHD. Fidgeting, constant running, being unable to play, and nonstop talking are all signs of hyperactivity and impulsivity.

People who don't understand the condition often say that a person with ADHD is acting out or is a troublemaker. They'll often categorize such a person as disorganized, careless, and lacking in social graces. They may say the person is rude or stupid. But these stereotypes are unfair. The truth of the matter is that people with ADHD can't help how they feel, any more than people with physical illnesses can help how they feel.

History of ADHD

Although the term *ADHD* is fairly new, the condition itself is not. But our understanding has evolved and improved over the years.

In 1798 a Scottish physician named Sir Alexander Crichton published a book that delved into the "nature and origin of mental derangement." In one chapter, "On Attention, and Its Diseases," he described a condition that

A portrait of Sir Alexander Crichton.

is very similar to what doctors today would call ADHD. Crichton said "abnormal inattention" will usually **manifest** "at a very early period of life, and has a very bad effect, inasmuch as it renders [a person] incapable of attending with constancy to any one object of education. But it seldom is in so great a degree as totally to impede all instruction; and what is very fortunate, it is generally diminished with age."

Crichton described those with such inattentiveness as having "mental restlessness." He wrote that some of his patients were easily excited by people walking or by "a slight noise" in the room. "Too much light, or too little light, all destroy constant attention in such patients."

In 1844 the German physician Heinrich Hoffman wrote a series of illustrated books for children, including stories about a character named "Fidgety Phil," whose behavior at the dinner table culminated in a big mess. Some researchers believe Hoffman was interpreting an early case of ADHD. "Let me see if Philip can be a little gentleman," the father in the book intones, "Let me see if he is able to sit still for once at the table."

Most experts say Sir George Frederick Still, who is often referred to as the father of British pediatrics, was the first modern doctor to truly understand ADHD. In a series of lectures presented to the Royal College of Physicians in 1902, Still told the stories of 43 children who had problems paying attention. They were often aggressive, emotional, and resistant to discipline. One of his patients, a "boy, aged 6 years . . . was unable to keep his attention even [while playing] a game for more than a very short time, and as might be expected, the failure of attention was very noticeable at school, with the result that in some cases the child was backward." But Still said that despite these attention problems, the boy, "in manner and ordinary conversation, . . . appeared as bright and intelligent as any child could be."

During the late 20th century, ADHD was known as hyperkinetic impulse disorder. In 1980, doctors changed the name to attention deficit disorder, or ADD. Experts created two subtypes of ADD: ADD with hyperactivity and ADD without hyperactivity.

Doctors found that children who had ADD but were not hyperactive were substantially different from children with ADD who were hyperactive. Doctors described ADD children without hyperactivity as "more day-dreamy, . . . lethargic, and disabled in academic achievement, but as substantially less aggressive and less rejected by their peers" than those with ADD with hyperactivity.

Different Types

ADHD, as we know it today, was finally defined by the American Psychiatric Association in 1987, and the definition has been further refined since then. Instead of two subtypes, there are now three forms of ADHD, depending on which symptoms are more prevalent. For example, those who find it hard to organize themselves or finish a job have *predominantly inattentive presentation* ADHD. Anyone who falls into this category can be easily distracted or forget routine details. They find it difficult to follow instructions or, in extreme cases, to hold a conversation.

Those with *predominantly hyperactive-impulsive presentation* might fidget a lot, talk incessantly, or find it hard to sit still for a protracted period. They'll take things away from others, and speak or shout out at the most inappropriate times. They seldom wait their turn. They often do not listen to or follow directions. They tend to be extremely impulsive. Smaller children with this disorder tend to be constantly on the run.

Combined presentation ADHD is the third subtype. People with combined presentation ADHD have the symptoms of both predominantly inattentive and predominately hyperactive-impulsive ADHD.

Other Problems

Nearly 75 percent of individuals with ADHD have at least one other coexisting mental condition, such as anxiety or depression. Some may also have a learning disability. According to the National Resource Center on ADHD, about 40 percent of those with ADHD have something called *oppositional defiant disorder*, or ODD. This condition is often marked by refusing to follow rules and a tendency to blame others for problems. People with ODD sometimes deliberately annoy others; they can be vindictive, resentful, and angry. Others might have *conduct disorder* (CD), in which they

"YOUR SON WILL NEVER BE ABLE TO FOCUS . . ."

Even as a kindergartener, Michael Phelps knew he was different. By the sixth grade, he'd been diagnosed with ADHD. The condition was so bad that a teacher once told his mother, "Your son will never be able to focus on anything."

As a teen, Phelps liked to be the center of attention. He was unruly and could be dangerously mischievous. One day in science class, he turned on all the gas burners in the laboratory just to irritate his classmates. When the school talent show came around, Phelps signed up to juggle, even though he didn't know how.

Luckily, Phelps discovered swimming. "Once I figured out how to swim, I felt free," he later recalled. "I could go fast in the pool, it turned out, in part because being in the pool slowed down my mind. In the water, I felt, for the first time, in control."

Although Phelps couldn't sit still in class, he was at home in the water. By the time he turned 10, he was ranked nationally. By the time he was 15, he was in the Olympics. For Phelps, the pool was a safe place where he excelled. Now, as an athlete who has won the most medals in Olympic history, Phelps's foundation helps kids with ADHD by letting them swim—just as he did when he was a child.

Pictured above: Michael Phelps at the 2016 Olympic Games.

It's common for people with ADHD to have mood disorders as well.

show signs of aggressiveness. Those with CD often steal from others. They tend to lie easily and may destroy property. Sometimes people with CD run away from home or skip curfews. (See chapter four for more information on both of these issues.)

Nearly 38 percent of ADHD patients have some type of mood disorder. Some suffer from depression, mania, bipolar disorder, and Tourette syndrome, a mental disorder that manifests itself with motor and vocal tics. In addition, more than half of adults with ADHD, and nearly a third of children with the condition, have anxiety disorders. They worry excessively and feel stressed. Others have substance abuse problems, or find they cannot sleep at night. In fact, 50 percent of parents of children with ADHD say their sons and daughters have difficulty falling and staying asleep.

Text-Dependent Questions

1. What are three symptoms of ADHD?
2. How many different subtypes of ADHD are there?
3. Who was the first physician to describe ADHD?

Research Project

Check out this website on ADHD, which is hosted by the Centers for Disease Control and Prevention: www.cdc.gov/ncbddd/adhd/prevalence.html. You will see three maps and statistics of the percentage of kids in the United States aged 4 to 17 diagnosed with ADHD for 2003, 2007, and 2011. Compare the statistics for the three years. What can you conclude? Write down your thoughts, using the statistics to back up your claims.

WORDS TO UNDERSTAND

chromosome: a threadlike structure in the nucleus of most living cells that carries genetic information.

cognitive: the process of knowing, which includes awareness.

estrogen: a female sex hormone.

genes: units of hereditary passed down from parents to their children.

introverted: reserved, withdrawn, or inward-looking.

neurological: having to do with the function and structure of the human nervous system.

CHAPTER TWO

Causes of ADHD

"When you live in total squalor—cookies in your pants drawer, pants in your cookies drawer . . . and apple seeds in your bed—it's hard to know where to look when you lose your keys. The other day, after two weeks of fruitless searching, I found my keys in the refrigerator on top of the roasted garlic hummus. I can't say I was surprised. I was surprised when my psychiatrist diagnosed me with ADHD two years ago, when I was a junior at Yale."

At that moment, Maria Yagoda became part of a small group of adults—around 5 percent—who have been diagnosed with ADHD. "As a fairly driven adult female who found the strength to sit through biology lectures and avoid major academic or social failures, I, too, was initially perplexed by my diagnosis," Yagoda wrote in an article for *The Atlantic* in 2013. "ADHD does not look the same in boys and girls. Women with the disorder tend to be less hyperactive and impulsive, more disorganized, scattered, forgetful, and **introverted**."

Although boys might see a decrease in symptoms at puberty, "the opposite is true for girls, whose symptoms intensify as **estrogen** increases in their system, thus complicating the general perception that ADHD is resolved by puberty," Yagoda continued.

As Yagoda says, ADHD is not the same for everyone. It affects males differently than females, and older people differently than younger people. But despite our understanding of its effects, just what causes ADHD remains a bit of a mystery. Evidence suggests that there are three main factors that somehow interact: genetics, brain development, and environment.

Genetics

One thing experts know for sure: the condition runs in families. In other words, **genes** play a role. Genes determine such inherited traits as the color of our eyes and hair, and they also play a role in what types of disorders we develop. A 2009 review of all the available scientific literature on ADHD concluded that genetics

WHAT ADHD IS NOT

People with ADHD
- are not lacking in intelligence or motivation,
- are not children of bad parents or teachers,
- are not faking a disorder,
- are not using the condition as an excuse to misbehave,
- do not have the illness because they consume too much sugar,
- do not have the illness because of allergies or hormones, and
- do not always "outgrow" the disorder (in fact, up to 30 percent of children with ADHD will have symptoms in adulthood).

plays a significant role in the development of ADHD, although it is hard to pinpoint which genes are to blame. Scientists have so far only linked one **chromosome** to ADHD, but they are still searching.

EDUCATIONAL VIDEO

Scan this code for a video about how it feels to have ADHD.

Scientists also know that if one parent has ADHD, there is a 30 percent chance that they will have a child with ADHD. If both parents have ADHD, the number increases to 50 percent. A younger sibling has more than a 30 percent chance of having ADHD if an older brother or sister has it. Moreover, chances that identical twins will have the condition are greater than the chances of fraternal twins, which scientists interpret as another indication that ADHD has a strong genetic component.

Brain Development

ADHD impacts several areas of the brain including the *prefrontal cortex*, which is responsible for **cognitive** behavior and decision making. The prefrontal cortex also influences how a person acts in social situations. ADHD also impacts the parts of the brain responsible for motor function and muscle activity. As a result, ADHD affects inhibition, memory, planning, motivation, and impulsivity.

Dr. Russell Barkley, an expert on ADHD, told *National Geographic* magazine that "the evidence is overwhelming that ADHD is the result of **neurological** factors and that these problems with brain development and functioning can arise from differences in genes that construct and operate the brain."

Researchers have noticed that the brains of people with ADHD look different from the brains of those without the condition. One 2013 study compared the

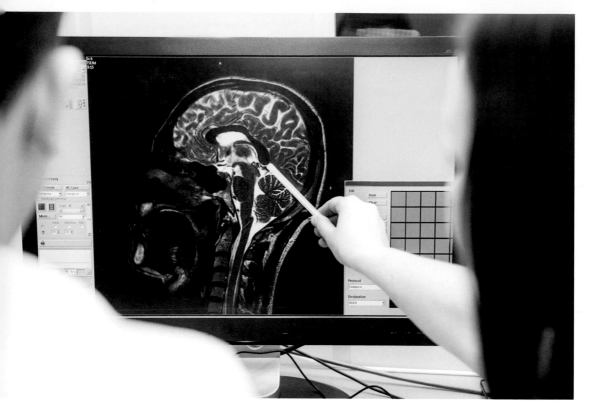

Researchers study brain scans to figure out if the brains of people with ADHD are different from those of other people.

brain scans of 29 adolescent boys with ADHD to the brain scans of 29 boys without ADHD. After comparing the scans, researchers were able to accurately tell (nearly 8 out of 10 times) which boys diagnosed with ADHD actually had the condition.

A study by the National Institutes of Mental Health concluded that certain sections of the brain mature more slowly in people with ADHD than in those without the condition. Much of this disparity occurs in the frontal lobe, the part of the brain that controls attention, planning, impulse control, and concentration.

Brain scans have also revealed that the front part of the brain is less active in children with ADHD than in those without ADHD. While this might seem contrary, it actually makes a lot of sense. Experts say that the front part of the brain calms the regions that deal with emotions, making it harder for people with ADHD to control their impulsiveness.

Research has also suggested that the brains of children with ADHD take a longer time to develop a so-called internal language, the "private voice" inside one's mind. We humans use this internal voice to talk to ourselves and make decisions. That voice, researchers say, is essential in how humans develop. The delay in hearing this voice causes problems for some people in following instructions.

Environmental Factors

Heredity does not tell the whole story of ADHD. Many researchers believe that ADHD results from environmental factors as well. Premature birth, low birth rate, tobacco smoking, and drinking alcoholic beverages during pregnancy have all been linked to ADHD in children. Exposure to heavy metals, chemicals, and other environmental factors may also play a role in ADHD cases.

In 2014, researchers at the CDC reviewed the scientific evidence to see if smoking during pregnancy increases the risk of ADHD in children. Although researchers could not find a direct link between smoking and ADHD, the CDC concluded that mothers who smoke are more likely to have children who develop disruptive behavior disorders. However, the idea was also raised that mothers who smoke might do so because it improves their ability to focus. In other words, it's possible that that smoking is a *symptom* of ADHD, rather than a cause. In any case, many of the studies researchers looked at had sample sizes that were very small, so nothing definitive could be assumed.

However, in 2016, researchers at Yale University concluded that nicotine—a toxin in cigarettes—can indeed impact the genetic makeup of an unborn child. Smoking while pregnant, the researchers warned, not only increases the risk of a child suffering from ADHD, but also increases the risk of addiction and behavioral problems later in life.

It's just not smoking that can have an impact. In 2016, researchers also announced that pregnant women who take acetaminophen, a drug found in over-the-counter pain and cold medicines, have a greater risk of their children developing hyperactivity or attention problems.

The researchers followed 14,000 pregnant women. They found that 53 percent used acetaminophen during their first 18 weeks of pregnancy, and that 43 percent of women used it during 32 weeks or more. After factoring in other potential causes for behavior problems, scientists found that pregnant women who used the drug during their first 18 weeks of pregnancy increased their chances of giving birth to a child with ADHD-like behaviors. Those who used acetaminophen for 32 weeks or longer put themselves at an even greater risk of having a child who had hyperactivity issues or emotional problems.

Smoking can change the genetics of an unborn child, which may make the baby more susceptible to ADHD.

Studies have also investigated whether exposure to alcohol during pregnancy can increase to the risk of ADHD. In 2002, researchers at Harvard Medical School reported that pregnant women who drink alcohol and smoke may double their chances of having their child develop ADHD. The team of researchers looked at the medical records of 280 children diagnosed with ADHD. After interviewing their mothers about their drinking and smoking habits, the researchers concluded that children diagnosed with ADHD were more likely to have been exposed to tobacco and alcohol before they were born. But again, this was a fairly small study, and studies that rely on the subjects' personal recollections are not necessarily definitive. The search for more definitive answers on the causes of ADHD will continue.

Text-Dependent Questions

1. How does genetics play a role in ADHD?
2. Which parts of the brain does ADHD impact?
3. Name two environmental factors that may play a role in ADHD.

Research Project

Research the regions of the brain and create a chart or graphic organizer showing the function of each region.

WORDS TO UNDERSTAND

neurotransmitters: chemicals in the body that move messages between nerve cells.

nominal: very small; token.

psychotropic: relating to drugs that affect a person's mental state.

CHAPTER THREE

Treating ADHD

Max Been was eight years old when he was diagnosed with ADHD. He had been struggling in school. He couldn't get his work done, and he was getting into an awful lot of trouble. His mother, Ali Farquhar, knew something wasn't quite right with Max long before he entered elementary school. His preschool teacher would phone her, wondering if Max had gotten enough sleep the night before. As school became more demanding, Max grew more impulsive and disruptive in class. Studying was also a huge challenge. He'd spend hours struggling to do his homework, only to write a few words.

One day, as Max was sitting in the back of the car driving past the firehouse, his mother asked: "If there were a pill that would help you focus better, would you be interested?" Max was. His doctor prescribed Ritalin, and the change, according to Max's mom, was instantaneous. "There was an immediate improvement," she said. "His teachers noticed a difference too."

"I could slow myself down," Max later told Lesley Alderman, a writer for *Everyday Health*. But Max understood that the medication was "not a miracle cure." "If something doesn't interest me, it's a titanic struggle for me to focus on it," he told Alderman. "The act of doing it is so unwelcome."

Positive Energy

Unlike a head cold or a skinned knee, ADHD doesn't go away on its own. But although there is no cure, the condition is treatable. The options are as varied as ADHD's symptoms.

The first step in coming to terms with ADHD is getting an accurate diagnosis from a doctor. Unlike most diseases and illnesses, there is no blood test, no X-ray, no MRI that can tell whether a person has ADHD. Doctors make their diagnosis by evaluating the patient, making subjective decisions based on their observations and screening questionnaires. A number of different professionals, including pediatricians, psychiatrists, and psychologists, are qualified to diagnose ADHD in both children and adults.

Not only does an accurate diagnosis open the door for the correct treatment plan, getting the news can also be therapeutic, because it finally puts a name to the problem.

Once a professional has correctly diagnosed ADHD, the next step for many health professionals is to find out the positive talents and strengths of the patient in order to help him deal with the illness. "If treatment is to be as transformative as possible, it must look for the treasures," note the authors of *Delivered from Distraction*. "It must ferret out the hidden strengths, the potential talents in every child . . . and in every adult. It must discover where the brain lights up."

Finding out what a person with ADHD is good at, and developing those talents, helps everyone, including parents and siblings, get into a positive frame of mind, because, as Hallowell and Ratey write, "without positive energy, treatment fails."

Behavioral Therapy

ADHD not only affects a person's ability to pay attention or sit still, it also affects relationships with family and friends. Behavioral therapy is a treatment option that can reduce the disruptiveness of ADHD. Some kids have a lot of success in managing their symptoms with behavioral therapy alone, but frequently doctors

Pediatricians are often the first professional parents talk to about ADHD symptoms.

will recommend a mixture of behavioral therapy and medication (medication is covered in the next section).

The first thing to understand about behavioral therapy is that it doesn't change the fundamentals of the person's condition. Behavior therapy doesn't make ADHD go away in the sense that, for example, an antibiotic makes an infection go away. Instead, behavioral therapy teaches people how to manage their symptoms. Behavioral therapy is about acquiring and practicing skills—organization, impulse control, anger management, and so on.

Parents play a critical role in behavioral therapy; in fact, a key segment of behavioral therapy is called "parent training," because kids with ADHD and their parents practice skills together. Parents learn new ways of relating to their kids with ADHD. For example, they need to make sure the kids clearly understand what is expected of them. Also, parents are taught to follow through consistently when it comes to both rewards and punishments.

One part of behavioral therapy for ADHD involves practicing skills that will help students be more successful at school.

A second key part of behavioral therapy involves what's called "executive functions." To understand what these are, picture the activities of someone who runs a small company, also called a "chief executive." She sets goals for her employees and makes sure they meet those goals, she creates a calendar of when certain tasks need to be completed, and

EDUCATIONAL VIDEO

Scan this code for a video about using behavioral therapy for ADHD.

she makes sure that her employees have the resources they need to do what she wants. Even though we aren't all executives, we do all need "executive functions" like organization, planning, and time management. For some people, these functions come naturally, but for others, they need to be learned. Behavioral therapy helps kids with ADHD acquire these skills. Kids practice using checklists and planners to keep organized, setting reasonable deadlines to get assignments done, and following step-by-step instructions to complete tasks such as math problems and essay writing.

Medications

"I sat down to work. I got up to get a glass of water and remembered an important bill I needed to pay, and logged into my bank's website to pay it. Before I'd finished that task, I gotten distracted by a book I've been meaning to review, sitting on the desk. Less than a chapter into the book I IM'd a friend with a question about plans for the weekend.

"And so it went, until I remembered a key detail: I had forgotten to take my Ritalin this morning. Now I've taken that little pill, and my workday has run

THE IMPORTANCE OF PRAISE

Experts say parents should praise their children five times more than they criticize them. There are a few reasons for this. First, we all tend to take criticisms to heart more easily than praise; it takes more praise to build someone up than it does criticism to take them down.

Also, kids with behavioral issues find themselves criticized *constantly*. Some days it seems like every move they make, from the classroom to the playground to the dinner table, is totally wrong. And when they do the right thing—when they sit still in class, for example— nobody notices, because that's what everybody else was already doing. Behavioral therapists believe that taking notice when a kid succeeds, even in small ways, is a key part of helping that kid learn to substitute a positive behavior for a negative one.

smoothly since. Is it really so simple? Sometimes, yes. Drugs can be the answer. Or at least part of the answer."

The blogger Sierra Black was first diagnosed with ADHD when she was in the first grade. She soon began taking an ADHD drug called Ritalin. The drug eased her symptoms and allowed her to focus. Ritalin gave Sierra the ability to pay attention and to sit still at her desk—not an easy feat, since she was more likely to crawl around the classroom floor.

As the years passed, Sierra went on and off the drug—"Until I wanted to go back to work. I realized quickly that I wouldn't be able to stick with a job without the help Ritalin had given me."

For many people, Ritalin, Adderall, and other ADHD drugs are miracle pills. Although they cannot cure ADHD, the drugs allow people to focus better than they ever could before. The drugs also help people to not act out in social situations.

Most ADHD drugs, including Ritalin and Adderall, are stimulants, a class of drugs that includes cocaine, methamphetamine, nicotine, caffeine, and a variety of prescription medications. Once inside the body, stimulants affect the brain by enhancing the effects of several key **neurotransmitters**, the chemicals that allow billions of brain cells to communicate with each other.

Specifically, stimulants enhance the effect of two neurotransmitters—dopamine and norepinephrine. Dopamine is sometimes called the "feel good" neurotransmitter. For many with ADHD, the medications improve the ability to

One piece of good news is that there's lots of information about ADHD available online. The more you know about your condition, the better equipped you'll be to handle it.

concentrate and control emotions. The medications also allow them to make and follow through on plans and projects.

For the medications to work, however, they must be taken as prescribed. The effects of ADHD often return once a person stops using the drugs. And the medications don't work for everyone. While some people might see dramatic improvements in their behavior, others see only **nominal** gains. ADHD drugs help about 70 percent of adults and 70 to 80 percent of children.

DIFFERENT FORMS OF ADHD MEDICATIONS

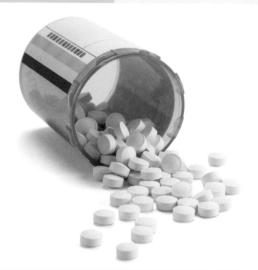

Most of the stimulants used to treat ADHD come in three forms: short acting, intermediate acting, and long acting. The short-acting medications must be taken two three times a day, while long-acting stimulants are not taken as often. Some of the most common stimulants for ADHD include:

- amphetamine sulfate (Evekeo)
- amphetamine/ dextroamphetamine (Adderall)
- dexmethylphendiate (Focalin, Focalin XR)
- dextroamphetamine (Adderall XR, Dexedrine, ProCentra, Zenzedi)
- lisdexamfetamine (Vyvanse)
- methylphenidate (Concerta, Daytrana, Metadate, Methylin ER, Quillivant XR, Ritalin)

A Raging Debate

ADHD drugs have become very controversial in recent years. Critics say doctors are overdiagnosing the condition and overprescribing stimulant medications. They believe children who are naturally high-spirited are being told they have a medical condition that they don't have. They also claim that when the diagnosis is correct, the children would be better served by other treatments, including diet and behavioral therapy.

Those on the other side of the debate say critics are exaggerating the number of incorrect diagnoses. People have become more aware of ADHD over time, and this greater knowledge may be responsible for an increase in the total number of cases. Moreover, they claim ADHD medications are safe and work better than all other treatments.

One thing is certain: since 1980, the number of ADHD cases diagnosed in the United States has skyrocketed. In fact, in 2011, researchers reported that 12 percent of U.S. children and teens had been diagnosed with ADHD. The number was staggering because the number of cases had increased by 43 percent from eight years earlier.

If those numbers, compiled by Sean D. Cleary, an associate professor of epidemiology and biostatistics at Milken Institute School of Public Health at the George Washington University, are to be believed, some 5.8 million children in the United States, ranging in age from 5 to 17, are living with diagnosed ADHD.

Although this study did not explain why the increase occurred, experts attribute the uptick in ADHD diagnosis to a variety of factors. For one thing, ADHD has become one of the most-studied pediatric conditions. Experts say that expanded awareness, better diagnostic techniques, and the passage of several U.S. laws, including the 1990 Individuals with Disabilities Education Act (IDEA), which recognized ADHD as a disability, have contributed to the rise in the number of cases.

Some experts say that ADHD is overdiagnosed, while others argue that the condition is just better understood.

Moreover, when Congress expanded Medicaid, a federal health-care program, for children in the 1990s, this opened the door to an increase in medical coverage for **psychotropic** medications. Psychotropic drugs affect a person's mental conditions. In the case of ADHD, those drugs were stimulants. Consequently, doctors began writing more prescriptions to treat ADHD. By 1996, doctors were writing four times as many prescriptions for ADHD as they did in 1987, and the number continued to increase through the 2000s.

In 2013 the *Wall Street Journal* presented a dueling op-ed piece laying out the controversy. For Dr. Sandy Newmark, head of the pediatric integrative neurodevelopment program at the University of California, San Francisco, the issue was simple. "There is no question that ADHD is a real disease that can have serious consequences," he wrote. "It is also true that medications can be of great benefit for certain patients with ADHD. But I also believe that ADHD is significantly overdiagnosed. And for those who do have the condition, medications aren't always the best or only option. . . . Simply put, this means that the people making the diagnoses aren't distinguishing, in many cases, between normal developmental immaturity and ADHD."

Harold S. Koplewicz, president of the Child Mind Institute in New York, countered by saying that ADHD is a real, widespread condition, and that the medications doctors prescribe are the most effective treatment. "For ADHD, the rate of diagnosis has gone up 3 percent to 5 percent a year, depending on the study," he wrote. "This isn't some grand delusion. It is the result of more parents and teachers recognizing the signs that certain children have serious problems concentrating, settling down and controlling their impulses. . . . It has been shown over and over again, in controlled scientific trials, that stimulant medication is the best and safest means of counteracting the symptoms of ADHD. As many as 80 percent of children respond well to one of these medications."

 ## ABUSING ADHD DRUGS

Some of the stimulants used to treat ADHD are being abused by people who do not have the condition but want to focus on their schoolwork. The illicit, nonmedical use of ADHD stimulants, especially Ritalin and Adderall, is second to only marijuana, according to researchers at the University of Michigan. At prices ranging from $5 to $20 a pill, the drugs are comparatively inexpensive and easy to obtain. Dealers sometimes steal the drugs from loved ones, lie to get prescriptions, or sell their own medications.

Changes in Lifestyle

Drugs and behavioral therapy are not the only ways to manage ADHD. Doctors also recommend that patients change their lifestyles. For example:

Teens with ADHD seldom get enough sleep. They stay up too late watching television or surfing the Internet, and then, in the morning, they have trouble

Phones and other devices can be terrible for sleep habits.

waking up. Various sleep disorders are associated with ADHD. You can improve your sleep by keeping to a regular schedule, staying away from caffeinated drinks, and banishing electronics from the bedroom.

Doctors have learned that one of the best treatments for ADHD is physical exercise (remember Michael Phelps from chapter one). Exercise can help the brain to focus.

For some people with ADHD, meditation, yoga, and prayer have positive effects. These practices focus the mind and have calming effects.

Diet plays a role, too. Anybody who doesn't eat properly can become easily distracted, restless, and impulsive. Although there is of yet no clear scientific connection between ADHD and certain foods, experts say that whatever is good for the brain is good for those with ADHD. High-protein diets that include cheese, eggs, meat, and nuts can improve concentration in everyone, and they could make ADHD drugs work more efficiently. Experts also say people, including those with ADHD, should cut down on candy, honey, sugar, and other simple carbohydrates, while loading up on vegetables and fruits, and on the omega-3 fatty acids found in fish and olive and canola oil.

Text-Dependent Questions

1. How does behavioral therapy work?
2. What are stimulants?
3. Why are some people concerned about ADHD medications?

Research Project

Use the Internet and the library to research a celebrity who has been diagnosed with ADHD. Prepare an oral presentation describing how ADHD impacted that person's life and what steps they took to overcome the condition.

WORDS TO UNDERSTAND

intermittent: periodic, not constant.

oppositional: taking a position of disagreement or resistance.

CHAPTER FOUR

Other Behavior Disorders

Because ADHD has a profound effect on the way people act, it's known as a behavioral disorder. Behavioral disorders cause impairments in people's ability to conform to our generally understood notions of "acceptable" behavior. For example, sitting still and listening to a teacher is widely accepted as the "correct" way to act in class. But, as discussed earlier, people with ADHD can find it very challenging to maintain that behavior for extended periods. When it comes to behavior disorders, it's not who the person is that causes the problem, it's the actions that the person takes.

ADHD is not the only type of behavioral disorder. It is the most common and, fortunately, the mildest. Other behavioral disorders, while more rare, can be more difficult to handle. They include **intermittent** explosive disorder, **oppositional** defiant disorder, and, most seriously, conduct disorder.

Intermittent Explosive Disorder

We have all "lost our cool" at one time or another. Even the most patient among us has had the experience of becoming so frustrated or upset that it feels like our brains shut down completely, and we just want to scream or throw something. The nature of our ire changes as we grow: little kids have tantrums, while their parents may have "road rage." It's not pretty, but it's human.

Sometimes these rages are caused by other emotional or physical problems, such as bipolar disorder or alcoholism. But when someone has loud, violent outbursts on a regular basis, with no clear cause, this may be a problem called intermittent explosive disorder (IED).

People with IED have trouble managing their aggressive impulses. They can be calm one minute and aggressive the next. Their rages can take a variety of forms. Some people will shout, scream, and rant. Others might become

Tantrums are a natural part of childhood, but it's expected that we'll grow out of them.

physically aggressive. They often break things or start fights. What sets IED apart from more "typical" anger issues is that the actions of someone with IED happen regularly, out of nowhere, and out of proportion with the situation. The smallest thing, such as losing a board game, can set them off. The good news is that intermittent explosive disorder is fairly rare. IED typically occurs in young men (under 35), and it's strongly associated with either an emotional or physical trauma in childhood.

EDUCATIONAL VIDEO

Scan this code for a video about childhood behavioral disorders.

Oppositional Defiant Disorder

You've probably met somebody who has trouble with authority. Whether it's a parent, a teacher, or a boss, some people really struggle to accept the idea that others can tell them what to do. This is not, in itself, a mental disorder—although it may make the person challenging to deal with! Oppositional defiant disorder (ODD) involves an intensely negative reaction to authority figures, but it goes beyond that.

People with ODD flout authority and often have a lot of trouble walking away from an argument, no matter how trivial. They will often blatantly refuse to follow instructions, and they also tend to blame others for their mistakes. ODD sometimes has a mood component as well as a behavior component. In other words, people with ODD tend to be in an irritated frame of mind a lot of the time, and they make an effort to irritate others, usually for no clear reason.

People with oppositional defiant disorder are not be able to walk away from a conflict, even when they know they should.

From the outside, it may seem as though people with ODD are determined to make everyone else as miserable as they are.

ODD can be mild, moderate, or severe—this is determined by the number of settings where the person tends to act out. It's common, for instance, for a teenager with mild ODD to take her anger out on their family at home, but not at school. The more settings in which the person acts out, the more severe their disorder is said to be. The most severe cases of ODD involve a person who is generally hostile in all situations.

Doctors don't know exactly what causes ODD, although the symptoms usually manifest themselves in childhood. Adults with ODD frequently also have drug and alcohol problems.

Conduct Disorder

We began this chapter by noting that people with behavioral disorders have trouble following the generally understood norms of certain "acceptable" behaviors. In the case of IED, people can't control their anger. People with ODD tend to feed off conflicts with other people. But the most troubling of all behavioral disorders is one in which people openly and frequently violate the basic rights of others. This is called conduct disorder. Typical behaviors of people with conduct disorder include threats as well as actual physical violence, bullying, lying frequently, stealing, and harming animals.

It's important to understand that even highly negative behaviors do not automatically mean someone has a contact disorder. Bullying is a perfect example. It's not okay for any reason, but the reality is that some kids do go through a phase of targeting people who seem weaker. But most of these kids know, deep down, that this behavior is wrong, and in time they will "grow out of it." This is the significant difference between a garden-variety bully and someone with conduct disorder. People with this disorder do not understand that their behaviors are wrong. As a result, they don't experience feelings of guilt or shame about their actions.

As with other behavioral disorders, we don't know precisely why someone develops a conduct disorder. It seems to involve a blend of hereditary and environmental factors. Some studies have also suggested that an injury to the part of the brain that handles impulse control may also be involved. As with IED, trauma in childhood may also play a role in some cases.

 GET TREATED

These behavior disorders may sound dire, but they are very treatable. For example, if treated, about 67 percent of people with ODD have no symptoms within three years.

ANGER MANAGEMENT

Here are some tips that anybody can try when they find themselves feeling angry:

- *Before you respond, pause.* When you get in a heated back-and-forth with someone, it's easy to simply say the first thing that springs to your mind. Instead, pause for a few seconds and check yourself—do you really want to say that?
- *Take a break.* If possible, step away from whatever situation is making you upset. Return to it when you have calmed down; you may see the same situation differently.
- *Don't "rehearse" your anger.* In other words, don't spend time going over and over your arguments as to why you are right and someone else is wrong. This isn't useful and will only make you more upset.
- *Fix the broken thing.* Instead of revisiting "your side" of the argument, try to focus on concrete actions you can take to make the situation better. It's possible that you and the other person will never agree, but you can still take steps to move forward and leave the argument behind.

Because the symptoms of conduct disorder often involve hurting others, it's very important that people with the disorder be treated. Most treatments for conduct disorder are psychological rather than pharmacological—there's currently no medicine that is approved to help people with this condition. Instead, the cognitive-behavioral therapies discussed in the previous chapter can help people with conduct disorder learn to manage their destructive impulses and find more productive outlets for angry feelings.

Bullying behaviors are one symptom of a possible conduct disorder.

Text-Dependent Questions

1. What's the difference between a garden-variety tantrum and IED?
2. Name three symptoms of ODD.
3. What percentage of people with ODD are symptom-free after three years of treatment?

Research Project

Find out more about anger management techniques. How do these techniques work? Make a list of some exercises and try them in your own life. Write about what you learned. Even if you don't have a behavior disorder, did you find that anger management helped you? Why or why not?

WORDS TO UNDERSTAND

exasperation: frustration.

obstinate: stubborn or inflexible.

rambunctious: high-spirited; lively.

CHAPTER FIVE

Living with Behavior Disorders

It's not easy living with a behavior problem, and it's not easy living with someone who has one, either. A parent or a guardian might not know exactly what is happening or what to do. Just ask Michelle Nielson, the stepmother of Chase, a boy who was diagnosed with ADHD in kindergarten.

"He wasn't like most kids who'd sit in their seat and follow directions," Nielson writes on the NBC News/Today Show website. "He was always getting time-outs, always in trouble because he couldn't control himself. He was hitting other kids. When you're told your kindergartner is suspended, it's devastating. We just thought, he's a **rambunctious** little boy."

When Chase was diagnosed with ADHD, Nielson and the child's mother wanted to put him on medication. To make matters worse, Chase had ODD, oppositional defiant disorder. "It was really hard to convince his dad—who wants to put their child on medication in kindergarten? But thank God for it. I never thought I'd say that, but to see Chase medicated and non-medicated, it's two different children. . . . He goes from bouncing up and down and not following directions . . . to being

Life at school can be tough for kids with behavior disorders, who may find themselves "in trouble" frequently.

focused and calm. He can process thoughts; he can do his homework. It's a whole different world."

Having a loved one with ADHD can be exhausting, exasperating, and at times embarrassing. Kids, by their very nature, tend to be active, rollicking, and impulsive. Sometimes they play too roughly or too loudly. They're careless and they lose things. They don't like to wait or to be told what to do. They can be **obstinate**. All of this is normal.

Now take what's normal for a child and amplify all of it by 10, 20, or 30 times if that child has ADHD. It's just not a bad day here or there. It's all the time, everywhere, everyday.

"School is the worst," Nielsen writes. "People treat a child in a wheelchair as disabled because they can see it. With a hidden disability, if you can't see it, [a lot of people think] it must not be real. What you see is the hyperactivity, the impulse-control issues. That all seems like a behavior issue. But underneath that . . . are learning disabilities, developmental delays, depression—so many other things going on that you don't see. You have to remember this is not his fault; he cannot control it. You want to protect your child, but have him held accountable for things, too."

What's a Parent to Do?

Once ADHD or any other behavioral disorder is diagnosed, it's the parents' job to help their child cope. Experts recommend telling children exactly what they have and how the condition affects mood and behavior. For the most part, kids with ADHD already know that something is "off," even if they don't know why. They see

Kids with behavior disorders need a lot of support from their parents.

the **exasperation** on other people's faces. They are constantly getting yelled at for doing something wrong. They often have a hard time reading, studying, or doing their homework. They may think they're stupid. They might think that everyone hates them. The more that people with ADHD can understand their condition, the better they will be at being kinder to themselves.

Among other things, experts recommend that parents spend extra time with their child. Children with ADHD, for example, often experience failure at a higher rate than others. Some of them don't get good grades. They may have trouble making friends. Experts say it's important for parents to be there for their children. If their child plays sports, parents should go to their games and stand and cheer. If they play in a musical recital, then clap the loudest.

Perhaps the most important thing parents can do for their child is to educate themselves. By expanding their knowledge, parents can try to understand how their children are feeling. It's also a good way to help other people understand the condition, especially siblings and grandparents.

What's a Kid to Do?

If you have been diagnosed with a behavioral problem, simply knowing why you are different can actually be a huge help. You might feel a huge sense of relief when you know what is ailing you. Putting a name to a problem, whether it's ADHD or some other disorder, lets a child know why he struggles at school, or why he is getting yelled at, or why it is so hard to make friends.

Moreover, knowing what's wrong gives a child a handle on what steps she can take to feel better. By putting a name to the problem, children can work with their parents and doctors to find a solution.

There is no simple explanation as to why behavioral disorders happen. As you read earlier, there are biological factors, psychological factors, social factors, and environmental factors. As discussed with ADHD, there are a number treatments that can help you, including medication and behavioral therapy, as well as learning about anger management and practicing behaviors that will help you get along better in a particular situation.

EDUCATIONAL VIDEO

Check out this video about living with ADHD.

The key is to take charge. A person with a behavior disorder has a problem, just like someone with a physical illness like the flu. Behavioral disorders may affect how you act, but they do not have to define who you are. With help, you can learn to modify your behavior and make better choices. While it might seem as if negative emotions are directing your every thought and action, it doesn't have to be that way.

An E-mail and Salvation

Kerri McKay didn't let her behavioral problem define who she was. In high school, she and her friends used to joke about "my ADHD." She had trouble remembering her locker combination. "I was constantly borrowing pencils because I never brought one to class." That was before Kerrie knew what was happening.

Kerri graduated from high school and went to college, where challenges mounted. Then, on a day when her professor was giving a Power Point presentation, he said something that changed her life. He asked the students to ask him for help with any of the mental health issues they were studying.

Kerri sat down at her computer and wrote her professor an e-mail, telling him what she was feeling. "With the one e-mail, I started my journey of being evaluated for learning and attention issues," she writes. "I learned that I have ADHD . . . the diagnosis changed my life for the better. After years of struggling in silence and feeling different, the biggest positive was understanding myself a lot better, and why I see the world the way I do."

ADHD and other behavior disorders can make academics more challenging, but they do *not* make success impossible.

Text-Dependent Questions

1. Name a few things that parents can do to help their children with ADHD.
2. How can ADHD cause problems for kids?
3. What is the importance of educating yourself about ADHD and other behavioral problems?

Research Project

Use the Internet, the library and other resources to create a public awareness poster about ADHD. Your poster should contain data and information about the condition as well as what students, parents, and teachers can do.

FURTHER READING

American Psychological Association. "Controlling Anger before It Controls You." http://www.apa.org/topics/anger/control.aspx.

Children and Adults with Attention-Deficit/Hyperactivity Disorder (CHADD). "About ADHD." http://www.help4adhd.org/Understanding-ADHD/About-ADHD.aspx.

Golden, Robert, Fred Peterson, and Karen Meyers. *The Truth about ADHD and Other Neurobiological Disorders.* New York: Facts on File, 2010.

Greene, Ross W. *The Explosive Child: A New Approach for Understanding and Parenting Easily Frustrated, Chronically Inflexible Children.* 5th ed. New York: Harper Collins, 2014.

Guare, Richard, Peg Dawson, and Colin Guare. *Smart but Scattered Teens: The "Executive Skills" Program for Helping Teens Reach their Potential.* New York: Guilford, 2012.

Shapiro, Lawrence E. *The ADHD Workbook for Kids.* Oakland, CA, Instant Help Books, 2010.

Taylor, John F. *The Survival Guide for Kids with ADHD.* Minneapolis, MN: Free Spirit Publishing, 2013.

WebMD. "ADHD in Children Health Center." http://www.webmd.com/add-adhd/childhood-adhd/default.htm.

Educational Videos

Chapter One: Watch Mojo.com. "Top 10 Inspirational People with ADHD." https://youtu.be/E6LxfDFSZ0s.

Chapter Two: PunDiddly. "Living with ADHD." https://youtu.be/_kt_hn5jRQ0.

Chapter Three: Howcast. "Behavior Therapy for ADHD." https://youtu.be/2ibSgOUigCE.

Chapter Four: Howcast. "Symptoms of Childhood Behavioral Disorders." https://youtu.be/MbuqHvbSnCQ.

Chapter Five: TedX Talks. "ADHD Sucks, but Not Really: Salif Mahamane." https://youtu.be/fWCocjh5aK0.

SERIES GLOSSARY

accommodation: an arrangement or adjustment to a new situation; for example, schools make accommodations to help students cope with illness.

anemia: an illness caused by a lack of red blood cells.

autoimmune: type of disorder where the body's immune system attacks the body's tissues instead of germs.

benign: not harmful.

biofeedback: a technique used to teach someone how to control some bodily functions.

capillaries: tiny blood vessels that carry blood from larger blood vessels to body tissues.

carcinogens: substances that can cause cancer to develop.

cerebellum: the back part of the brain; it controls movement.

cerebrum: the front part of the brain; it controls many higher-level thinking and functions.

cholesterol: a waxy substance associated with fats that coats the inside of blood vessels, causing cardiovascular disease.

cognitive: related to conscious mental activities, such as learning and thinking.

communicable: transferable from one person to another.

congenital: a condition or disorder that exists from birth.

correlation: a connection between different things that suggests they may have something to do with one another.

dominant: in genetics, a dominant trait is expressed in a child even when the trait is only inherited from one parent.

environmental factors: anything that affects how people live, develop, or grow. Climate, diet, and pollution are examples.

genes: units of hereditary information.

hemorrhage: bleeding from a broken blood vessel.

hormones: substances the body produces to instruct cells and tissues to perform certain actions.

inflammation: redness, swelling, and tenderness in a part of the body in response to infection or injury.

insulin: a hormone produced in the pancreas that controls cells' ability to absorb glucose.

lymphatic system: part of the human immune system; transports white blood cells around the body.

malignant: harmful; relating to tumors, likely to spread.

mutation: a change in the structure of a gene; some mutations are harmless, but others may cause disease.

neurological: relating to the nervous system (including the brain and spinal cord).

neurons: specialized cells found in the central nervous system (the brain and spinal cord).

occupational therapy: a type of therapy that teaches one how to accomplish tasks and activities in daily life.

oncology: the study of cancer.

orthopedic: dealing with deformities in bones or muscles.

prevalence: how common or uncommon a disease is in any given population.

prognosis: the forecast for the course of a disease that predicts whether a person

with the disease will get sicker, recover, or stay the same.

progressive disease: a disease that generally gets worse as time goes on.

psychomotor: relating to movement or muscle activity resulting from mental activity.

recessive: in genetics, a recessive trait will only be expressed if a child inherits it from both parents.

remission: an improvement in or disappearance of someone's symptoms of disease; unlike a cure, remission is usually temporary.

resilience: the ability to bounce back from difficult situations.

seizure: an event caused by unusual brain activity resulting in physical or behavior changes.

syndrome: a condition with a set of associated symptoms.

ulcers: a break or sore in skin or tissue where cells disintegrate and die. Infections may occur at the site of an ulcer.

INDEX

Illlustrations are indicated by page numbers in *italic* type.

ABOUT THE ADVISOR

Heather Pelletier, Ph.D., is a pediatric staff psychologist at Rhode Island Hospital/Hasbro Children's Hospital with a joint appointment as a clinical assistant professor in the departments of Psychiatry and Human Behavior and Pediatrics at the Warren Alpert Medical School of Brown University. She is also the director of behavioral pain medicine in the division of Children's Integrative therapies, Pain management and Supportive care (CHIPS) in the department of Pediatrics at Hasbro Children's Hospital. Dr. Pelletier provides clinical services to children in various medical specialty clinics at Hasbro Children's Hospital, including the pediatric gastroenterology, nutrition, and liver disease clinics.

ABOUT THE AUTHOR

John Perritano is an award-winning journalist, writer, and editor from Southbury, CT. He has written numerous articles and books on a variety of subjects including science, sports, history, and culture for such publishers as Mason Crest, National Geographic, Scholastic and Time/Life. His articles have appeared on Discovery.com, Popular Mechanics.com, and other magazines and Web sites. He holds a Master's Degree in American History from Western Connecticut State University.

PHOTO CREDITS